Children's Rooms

Homes & Ideas

Children's Rooms

Annie Ashworth

BOXTREE

Welcome to the *Homes & Ideas* book of *Children's Rooms*. *Homes & Ideas* is the magazine for bright, creative and budget-conscious home style, and is absolutely packed with informative and inspiring ideas. Lifestyles and homes are constantly changing, and with them are the needs of our readers. More ideas, more information and more easy-to-follow projects are always in demand, and it was this demand which has prompted the idea of a series of books covering in greater detail the most popular topics featured in *Homes & Ideas*. When it comes to decorating a child's room you can really go to town with colour and ideas – and even relive your own childhood loves and passions. *Children's Rooms* not only includes pages of bright and inspiring ideas to help you achieve this but also looks at the safety and practical aspects which are essential considerations. Ideas that will grow with your child are as important as creating a calming haven for a small baby and all these topics have been covered, so whether your children are still in cots or struggling with homework you will find lots of inspiration. *Children's Rooms* is the perfect partner for *Homes & Ideas* and will help insure that your child will be delighted with its new room – wherever you live.

Debbie Djordjevic
Editor – *Homes & Ideas*

Contents

Introduction

There is no room that is as much fun to decorate as a child's. You can follow tradition by choosing gentle, soft pastels, that will create a soothing relaxed atmosphere for the new baby. Or you can throw convention to the wind, and mix bold colours and patterns which will create a stimulating environment. Let your imagination run riot: here you have a marvellous excuse to be more creative with paints and fabrics than you would ever dare to be in the rest of the house.

A child's room reflects a growing personality: the changing mat and cot disappear; nursery rhyme friezes give way to crayoned masterpieces stuck to the wall. Before you know it, you are having to hide your disapproval of posters featuring strange looking pop stars whose music blares out late into the night. You may even be banned from the room altogether!

This book will help you to plan a child's room, from the beginning. There is advice on safety, ideas for decorating in a fresh and original way, and tips to help you get it right first time so you don't make expensive mistakes.

We'll help you to make the transitions from baby to school-age child to teenager. There's also a chapter full of ideas on decorating details and accessories which will help you to create a room that you'll be proud of and your child will love.

NOTE: I have used the masculine pronoun throughout the book when referring to children generally, to avoid the clumsy use of 'his or her'. No sexism intended!

1 A starting point

Well before your baby arrives, it is worth thinking about where it will sleep. By the end of your pregnancy, you'll be too big to enjoy dragging around shops looking at fabrics and wallpapers. It's possible that the room you have chosen will need attention from a builder or electrician, and the whole process may take longer than you imagined. You don't want to be rushing off to hospital with the paint still wet, and the curtains yet to be made!

The position of the room in the house is important. Though you may well have the baby in a crib in your room in the early weeks, eventually he will need a room of his own. Make sure that this room is near to yours so that you can hear the baby when he cries, and that it is not too far to drag yourself from a warm bed.

Choose a light airy room if possible, and before you start to decorate and spend any money, plan for the future. Make sure that the room is big enough for your child to grow up in, if you intend that to be his room for a while. If you are planning to have more than one child, you could use a smaller room for the nursery, decorated in a more babyish theme, and move the toddler into a larger room as he grows (perhaps when he graduates into a bed), or once the new baby arrives. Young children do not get attached to rooms when they are very young, and a young child would enjoy creating a bedroom with you.

Safety

Safety is the number one priority when planning a nursery. Even a very young baby can get into danger, by rolling over on a changing mat or grabbing at a mobile over his head. Once a child is crawling, an entirely new set of dangers appear, and it is worth making sure the room is accident-proof right from the start.

Electricity
• Ensure that plug sockets are tightly fixed to the wall and covered with plastic covers. Once a child is crawling, don't leave lights, heaters, etc., plugged in when not in use.
• Hide flexes and leads out of the way. They can be grabbed even by very young children.

Windows
• Use safety glass for low-level panes, and install vertical bars, which can be detached easily in an emergency.
• If you have double glazing, ensure that it too can be removed easily in an emergency.

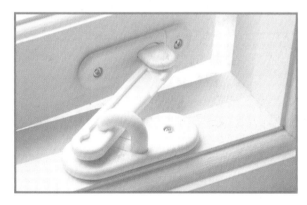

• Fit windows with safety catches so that they cannot be opened far enough for a child to squeeze through.
• Don't position a chair under a window, as a child might use it to climb up.

Furniture
• Choose furniture which has surfaces which can be wiped clean using anti-bacterial spray, especially around the changing mat area.
• Fix freestanding wardrobes or bookcases to the wall.
• Use only lead-free paint on walls, and non-toxic paint on furniture.

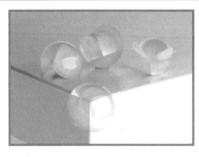

• Make sure that woodwork is rounded at the edges and not splintered. If necessary, use edge protectors.

• Use mirror plates to secure any pictures that are within reach of the child's cot.

Temperature

• Avoid overheating a nursery. Keep the temperature at 18°C, using a thermostatically controlled heater if necessary.

• Fit radiators and heaters with guards. Never use paraffin or oil burning heaters in a child's room.

Cot

• Buy a sturdy cot with no sharp edges, approved to British Standard 1753. The space between the cot bars should be 37–50mm.

• The cot mattress should fit snugly and be approved to British Standard 7177 and 1877.

• Never place a baby's bouncy chair or recliner on a bed or sideboard where it could fall off.

• Avoid positioning a mobile directly above a child's head where it may fall or be grabbed (over a cot or changing mat).

Essential equipment for a nursery

Expectant parents are always keen to get things right for their new baby, and baby equipment companies are not slow to persuade you that you simply cannot survive without this gadget or that device. The baby care market is huge, and more products appear all the time. But beware, there are a few essentials, the rest are a luxury. You will need:

1. Somewhere for the child to sleep. In the early days, this might be a Moses basket on a stand, or a crib, which can be kept close to your bed. A carrycot which is integral with your pram would be just as good. Alternatively, you could put a baby in a cot right from the start.

2. Somewhere to change his nappy. A foam-filled, plastic-covered changing mat is the best option. It is soft for the baby to lie on, and can be wiped clean with an anti-bacterial cleaner. (A terry towel laid under the baby will stop the mat feeling cold on his skin.) Place the mat on the floor, or on top of a sturdy chest of drawers at waist height for your comfort. Never leave a baby unattended on a mat, even for a moment.

3. Somewhere to store nappies and creams. This might be in a drawer or on an open shelf.

4. Hygienic nappy bin.

5. Low easy chair or nursing chair in which you will be comfortable when feeding the baby.

6. Clock for timing feeding sessions.

7. Lights (see page 12).

8. Storage for clothes.

9. Baby listening device for when you are out of earshot.

10. Pictures. Tiny babies can only focus on things very close to them, but their ability to see their surroundings develops very quickly.

Decorating basics

Paint and wallpaper

Any paint used in a child's room should be lead-free and non-toxic. Most modern paints are lead-free, but always check with the supplier. Emulsion and especially eggshell paints wipe clean very well when sticky fingers or pens have found their way onto them. It is easier to repaint a room than to re-paper it. If you do choose to hang wallpaper, a small-scale print is easier to live with. Paper should be stuck on well, because little fingers always manage to find a place where it can be pulled off.

Though bright colours can be stimulating for a child, you are likely to tire of them more quickly than neutral colours. Painting the walls light or mid-tone may be the answer, with decorative friezes (see Chapter 2) or any number of fun pictures or posters to provide the colour. These can be changed as the child grows.

Flooring

The floor should be non-slip, warm underfoot, easy to clean and durable. Choose dark-coloured carpet, as light colours soon become stained in a small child's room. Consider using carpet tiles which can be moved round if you need to hide stains. Cushioned vinyl or cork can be cleaned easily and covered with rugs, stuck down with adhesive tape. Position rugs next to the changing mat and other places which will take a lot of use.

Windows (See page 9 for safety tips)

You can have fun with styles of curtain and fabrics in a child's room. Use thick interlined fabric whenever possible to keep warmth in and to block out early morning light (and early morning waking). A blackout blind will block light very effectively during the summer months.

Lighting/plug points

Ceiling lights or wall-mounted lights are safer than lamps. If you do choose table lamps, choose 40W bulbs and make sure the flexes are hidden. Dimmer switches can provide restful light for the child, while still giving enough light to see to his needs when necessary. Consider a nightlight (lights within plugs work very well), which will enable you to see when you go to the child in the night, and will be useful until he is much older and confident in the dark.

When putting in plug points, make sure you have catered for nightlights, bottle warmer, heaters and fans which you may need. Think too about the future, when your child may need sockets near a desk next to the window.

Storage space used for nappies and creams can be transformed into shelving for toys and books as your child grows.

Furniture/Storage

There is a wide range of ideas for furniture and storage in the next chapter, but it is worth remembering the following points.

• Scaled-down furniture is expensive and not practical in the first year.

• Furnishings take quite a beating, so make sure chair covers are protected with fabric protector, and that cushion covers, curtains, etc., are machine-washable.

• Although clothes and toys take up very little room in the early days as babies grow, so do their clothes, toys and books. So plan cupboards and shelving which will serve you for a good few years to come.

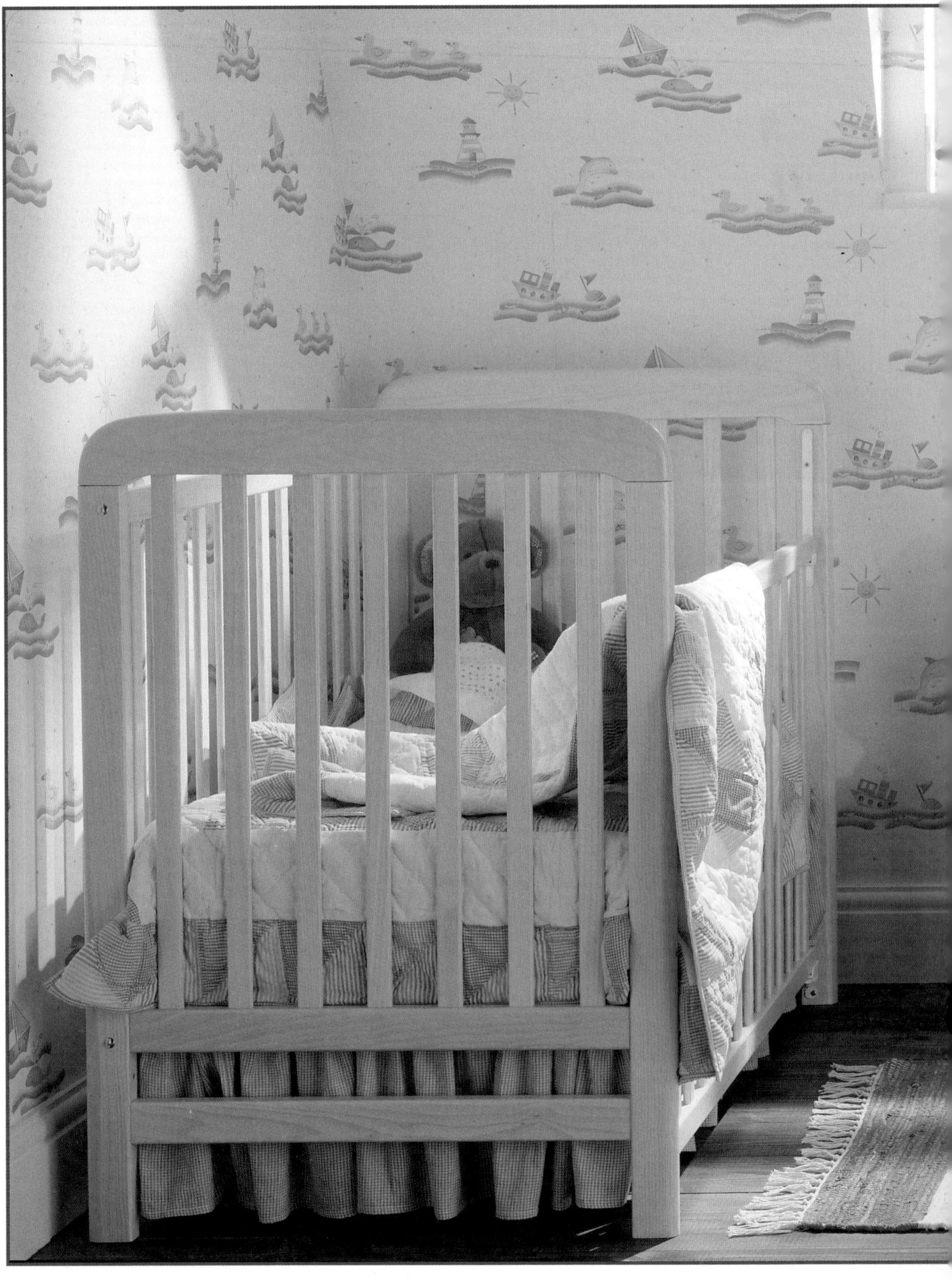

The asthmatic child

An alarming number of children have asthma these days. Though this may be due to smoking and pollution, allergy to the house mite is one of the biggest contributing factors. Unfortunately, house mites thrive on the centrally heated, cosy, carpeted environment we enjoy so much. If your child is asthmatic, or may have a predisposition to be (if you or your partner suffer) the following guidelines may be helpful.

• Where possible, use a mite-proof mattress, pillow and duvet cover. These are available through a number of outlets, including your local chemist, and vary enormously in price. Make sure that the mattress cover envelops the mattress completely. There is no conclusive evidence as to whether feather-and-down fillings or man-made fibres are preferable, but babies should not have pillows anyway, and it is easier to control a baby's body temperature with sheets and blankets than duvets. For an older child, hollow-fibre duvets can be machine-washed, which makes them the most practical.

• Avoid curtains, which collect dust, and therefore become mite traps. Blinds are better.

• Avoid carpets completely. Cover the floor with varnished wood or vinyl, which can be wiped with a damp cloth, and washable rugs.

• Make sure that furniture is painted or varnished so that it can be wiped with a damp cloth.

• Store toys and books in boxes where they will not become a dust trap.

• Keep soft toys to the minimum, and put them in the freezer once a month for at least 6 hours to kill the mite. Vacuum the toy after freezing to remove the mite faeces which is the allergen.

• Try to adopt a Scandinavian minimalist style, with as few 'frills' as possible. Lacy lampshades, cushions, etc., are very good dust traps.

2 Decorating the nursery

The good news is that there is no end to the number of fabric books, swatches, paint samples, and friezes to help you plan the decoration for the nursery. The bad news is that babies and young children are blissfully unaware of interior design, as long as they feel comfortable and secure. So, a beautifully co-ordinated nursery is really only a pleasure for you.

Of course, there is nothing wrong with wanting to create a beautiful environment for your baby, but don't be seduced into spending a lot of money on unnecessary extravagances. Think carefully about just how long a nursery-rhyme or teddy design will appeal to a growing toddler.

Anyone with a little patience can transform a baby's room by painting a mural or applying a stencil design around and down the walls. This is easy to do, and is a lot less expensive than buying ready-made friezes. (See page 58 and Chapter 5 for guidelines on painting and stencilling.)

Choosing the colour scheme

The advantage of a muted, pastel colour scheme is that you will not tire of it easily. Soft yellow walls (always a good option when you don't know the sex of the baby you are expecting!) or relaxing greens are easy to live with, and sit well with whatever you want to put with them. Cream too is warmer than white, and gives you free rein with the curtains, blinds and soft furnishings, which can be changed without you having to re-paint the walls.

You can be braver with colour in a child's room, even if you feel the need to be sensible in the rest of the house. The rule is that the bigger the room the better it can carry darker, bolder colours; though ochre yellows or lavender blues can make a small room look very cosy, especially when matched with greens and creams. Rich, jewel colours (emerald, jades and cerise pinks) can be stunning, especially when contrasted with white furniture and good light-

ing. Some colours can be very oppressive: avoid purples, deep blue/greens on walls. However the dark-green cot looks good here (**above**) because it is lifted by the yellow walls. Candy pinks and hard lemon yellows can be harsh, but well chosen fabrics will tone them down. Greens will soften pinks and yellows, and it is wise to choose a multi-coloured fabric that incorporates your strong colours within it.

Choosing fabrics

The more grown-up the fabric you choose, the longer it will be suitable and the more economical it will be. You might want to try stripes, or any number of ginghams or tartans, which are always fresh-looking and will not look too babyish as the child grows, especially if he will be using the room for years. Sprigged fabrics or soft florals are always attractive, and there is no point in being restricted too much by the sex of your baby: boys are just as happy with flowers as girls are with stripes!

Wallpapers and fabrics featuring a currently popular cartoon character are fun for a while, but babies will be non-the-wiser and toddlers are very fickle. Just as you have decorated the room in the latest thing, they will have moved onto the next fad. If a character theme appeals, plump for an image that has stood the test of time: such as rabbits, cows, tractors, Winnie the Pooh, or Beatrix Potter. A nursery-style theme is more practical if the room is likely to be used for second and/or third children.

Babies love the bright colours of bold fabric patterns. Choose classic images which have stood the test of time.

Choosing furniture

It is very tempting to fall in love with scaled-down chairs and tables, but, attractive though it is, miniature furniture is of little use in the first year. Any furniture you choose must be practical and easy to clean (see page 9), but it can still be fun as well as functional.

Baby clothes tend to fold rather than hang, so a sturdy chest of drawers is a useful investment. Place a changing mat on top, and, as long as the chest is at a comfortable height for you, it can be used as a nappy changing area. Simple shelves hung at eye level can be used to store muslin squares, nappies and creams. Later, the chest can revert to a dressing table, and the shelves can be used for books and oddments. It is worth storing nappies out of their bag to avoid having to fumble inside the pack when the baby is waiting on the changing mat.

If you want to hang dresses, a run of wooden pegs serves very well, as does a single wooden rail set under a shelf. The rail becomes useful for hanging toys, bags, etc., later on, when a wardrobe becomes essential.

The nursery chair must be comfortable for you to sit in when feeding or nursing your baby. Make yourself comfortable in a furniture showroom, and don't be put off by looming salespeople. Make sure the height is correct, so that your feet rest flat on the floor, with your knees at a 90° angle. Low arms for resting your elbows are a good idea, as is a rocking chair with a well balanced action.

If there is space, you may want to include a single bed into which the child will eventually grow. Keep the bed made up so it will be ready if you want to sleep in the room if your baby is ill or difficult to settle. Cover it in a pretty, washable quilt and decorate it with colourful cushions or soft toys so that it makes a comfortable place for you to sit and feed the baby.

The shelving unit in the baby's room provides a place to store small toys as well as nappies and changing accessories, and simple wooden pegs are used to hang a pretty dress. An easy and economical wardrobe has been made by hanging curtains and a simple squared pelmet from a chipboard or plywood shelf. The soft beige and pink colour scheme make this a very restful room.

COVERING HANGERS

Very few baby clothes need to be hung up, so a few dresses or jackets can be hung on the back of a door or on pegs or a single rail. Make them look more attractive by covering child-sized wooden hangers with a fabric which suits the room. You will need:

    child-sized hangers
    fabric
    medium-weight wadding
    strong adhesive
    sticky tape

1. Cut a thin strip of fabric 1.5cm wide, long enough to wind round and cover the hanger hook. Apply glue to the hook, fold the strip in half lengthways (wrong sides together) and wind it around the hook, starting and finishing at the bottom, and securing the ends around the hanger itself.
2. Wind the wadding around the hanger and fasten with sticky tape.
3. Cut a rectangle of fabric 2cm longer than the length of the padded hanger, and wide enough to wrap around it, adding 2cm seam allowance. Turn in a 1cm seam along all four edges.
4. Fold the fabric in half lengthways, wrong sides together, place the hanger in the fold, and stitch the ends together. Pin and slipstitch along the top of the hanger, tucking in the edges and neatening the fabric as you go.
NOTE: For a pretty finishing touch, tie a small bow of contrasting ribbon around the bottom of the hook.

Good quality traditional furniture, and classic fabric patterns are an excellent investment. They last well and will not be too babyish as the child grows up.

This soft fabric caterpillar will look marvellous on a nursery wall, keeping toys tidy in its pockets.

Choosing soft furnishings

Whether you decide to decorate your baby's room with soft pastels and lace, or bright colours and images, your added touches can make it an interesting place for him.

A good number of companies include wallpaper, friezes, curtains, cot quilts, cot bumpers and cushions in a nursery 'package'. This takes the donkey work out of decorating at a time when your energy may be low, and it can be more economical too.

If you would rather put together a more eclectic selection, pick out the fabric or wallpaper which appeals most, and then select a plain colour for the walls or curtains. You may want to add cushions which contrast: stripes with gingham or floral curtains for example. If you intend your child to stay in the room as he grows, why not choose neutral curtains and wallpaper, which aren't too babyish, and be a little more whimsical with the quilt fabric on the cot, or the scatter cushions? Details such as pictures, mobiles and lampshades can be changed as the child grows up.

> **WARNING**
>
> Cot bumpers could be a choking hazard if a baby was to get his head trapped underneath. Make sure they are tied very securely and removed once a baby is able to roll over on his own.

The nursery for twins

Your life will be easier if you keep both twins in the same room. Very small babies rarely disturb each other when they cry, and, although having twins does mean a certain amount of doubling up, putting them together will keep that to the minimum. In terms of decorating and equipment, everything is as it is for one baby (one changing mat will do) but you will need to think about:

• a room big enough for two growing people
• two cots
• two nursing chairs, for two people to feed the twins at the same time
• extra storage space for more nappies
• a larger nappy bin
• more space for storing clothes (wardrobe with shelves on one side would be practical now and in the future)
• two bouncy chairs for when the babies are awake and playful, and a soft quilt where you can lie one baby safely whilst seeing to the other
• keeping some changing things in the living room, to save leaving one baby unattended whilst seeing to the other

NOTE: As twins grow they tend to help each other in mischief, so ensure that you are especially careful about safety!

• Babies love to have something to look at. Make your own pictures by cutting out images from wrapping paper or posters, and placing them in ready-made colourful frames which are inexpensive and easy to find. As the child grows you can change the images.

• Babies love to look at themselves, so place a special baby's safety mirror in his cot, or fix one to the wall (with mirror plates) next to his changing mat. Once the baby is crawling, fix a mirror at floor level, and watch him try to look behind it to find that other baby!

• Avoid the danger of plastic bags by keeping cotton wool close by in a basket. You could also line the basket with the same fabric as used for the curtains.

• Store baby toys and first books in a large basket on the floor. This makes them easier to tidy away but easy for a sitting baby to reach. Make sure the basket has no sharp edges. A play-pen is always useful as a toy store, but, more importantly, it is a safe place to put a mobile baby if you need to leave the room for any reason.

Mobiles delight very small children, and need not be complicated or expensive. All that is required is a few interesting shapes and colours (even kitchen whisks or cotton reels tied securely to a coat hanger would do). A light mobile hung near an open window will dance in the breeze.

For a card or wooden mobile you will need:

- thin white paper
- thick card or balsa wood (available from model shops)
- scissors or scalpel
- gimlet for making holes
- oil-based paints or brightly coloured paper
- about 60cm of wooden dowel
- small saw
- thick cotton thread

1. From a book, choose one or two simple shapes, such as stars, hearts, crescent moons, ducks, teddies.
2. Trace the shapes onto the plain white paper and cut them out to make templates. Draw round the templates onto the card or balsa wood, to make 5 shapes.
3. Cut out the shapes using scissors or a scalpel, depending on the medium you are using, and make a small hole at the top of each shape with the gimlet.
4. Decorate the shapes by sticking coloured or reflective paper on both sides, or by painting. Always wait until one colour of paint has dried before applying the next (to dry them without smudging, peg them to a washing line or drying rack). Keep the detail simple if you are not a confident painter.

5. Using the saw, cut the dowel into three pieces: one piece 30cm long, and two pieces 15cm long. Cut two pieces of thread the same length (about 15cm) and tie one to each end of the longest piece of dowel. Tie a small length of dowel centrally to the end of each piece of thread.
6. Cut four more pieces of thread (15 or 20cm long, depending on the final length of the mobile, remembering that the baby must not be able to grab it) and attach these to the four ends of the shorter lengths of dowel.
7. Lie the mobile on a flat surface and carefully tie on the finished, dry shapes, pushing the thread through the holes you have made.
8. To hang the mobile, tie a piece of thread as long as required to the centre of the longest piece of dowel, and hang it from a hook or small screw in the ceiling (never a drawing pin). Never hang a mobile directly over a baby's head.

Other ideas:

You may want to use shapes made out of fabric – felt is ideal as it doesn't fray. Simply fold the fabric in two, right sides together, and draw the shape onto the wrong side of the fabric with tailor's chalk, adding 1cm for a seam. Cut out the shape through both pieces of fabric, and stitch a 1cm hem, leaving a 3cm opening for turning. Turn the shape right sides out, and fill with kapok or a man-made filling. Fold in the opening and hand stitch the edges together. Make up the mobile in the same way as above, and attach the shapes by using a needle to pass thread through the top of the shape.

These soft shapes can also be used on their own to decorate a curtain pelmet or a wall (see page 60).

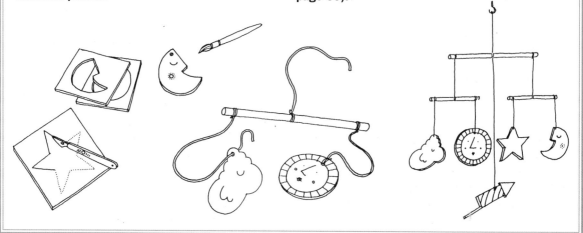

Once small children become aware of their surroundings, at around 5 or 6 months, they will love the bright colours and simple images of a mural. Don't be put off by the idea that murals are difficult to do, they are only as complicated as you make them. Pick an image which will interest your child until he is four or five. Soldiers, teddies, flowers, farmyard animals, are all classic images whose appeal will not wane. There are two ways to paint a mural:

1. Copy a picture freehand in pencil on a flat, prepared area of wall. You may have to keep rubbing out your mistakes, but this will not show once you start to paint the picture. Use the wall preparation method and paint recommendations outlined below.

2. If you are less confident of your artistic abilities, draw a grid over the original picture you have chosen, construct a larger grid on the wall, and transfer the design to the wall, square by square. The number of grid squares needed will depend on how complicated your chosen design is.

You will need:
• for the base colour and the picture use either all oil or all water-based paints
• drawing materials
• tracing paper
• ruler and T-square
• plumb line (string and a blob of Blu-Tack will do) and spirit level
• very soft pencil, charcoal or chalk
• brushes (in a variety of sizes)
• acrylic non-yellowing varnish for water-based paints or oil-based varnish for oil-based paints

1. Prepare the wall. It should be smooth, clean and have at least two layers of paint to ensure that it is non-absorbent. Gloss is not suitable and oil-based paint is preferable.

2. Choose the image you want to copy and draw a squared grid over it onto tracing paper, labelling the squares with letters across and numbers down, like a map reference. Use a ruler and T-square to ensure that the grid is straight and square.

3. Transfer the grid to the wall, scaling up the size of the squares perhaps 1:10 (if the squares on your drawing measure 1cm, the squares on the wall would measure 10cm). The amount you scale up will depend on how big you want the picture. Use a plumb line, spirit level and ruler to ensure that the grid is straight and square.

4. Mark out the design on the wall, using a very soft pencil or charcoal, or use chalk if your base colour is dark. Transfer each square one at a time, referring constantly to the original.

5. Working with the paints, fill in the colour, starting with the largest areas of colour and working from the top of the picture to avoid smudging. Always use a stepladder rather than reaching too high. Make sure one colour has dried before you start another, especially if they are next to each other. Some colours may need two coats. If you make a mistake, leave it to dry, and paint over it later.

6. You might want to finish the picture by adding a sharp black outline using a thin brush, or felt-tip pen. Choose a paint or ink which is compatible with the varnish.

7. Before sealing the mural with varnish, make sure the paint is completely dry, and rub out any visible grid lines or pencil mistakes.

3 The growing child

Once a child is able to walk, and moves from a cot to a bed, he will be able to enjoy and make the most of his environment. Small children love to be where you are, and they do manage to spread mess all around the house, but if their bedroom is an interesting and stimulating place to be, they will want to spend many hours playing there.

Try to create an environment where the pre-schooler can relax and play without feeling that his bedroom must always be spick and span. It is highly likely that his bedroom will also be his playroom, and, if you plan well, toys don't take long to clear up. He is less likely to create mess or damage furniture and fabrics if you set aside an area with a washable floor for activities such as drawing, or using crayons and playdough. Otherwise you may have to restrict them to the kitchen table!

As your child grows, he will still want to play, though in a less messy and more constructive way, and he will also need a place for doing homework.

Making the transition

If you plan ahead, the transition from nursery to bedroom shouldn't be difficult or expensive. You may want to save the cot for the next baby, or you could buy a cot which transforms into a bed, saving an extra purchase.

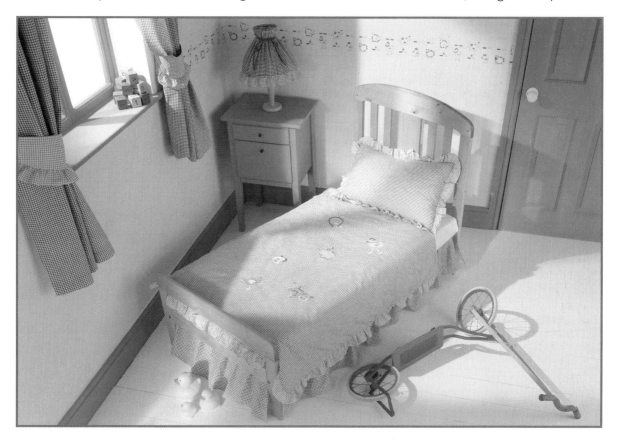

Every child will eventually need a full-sized bed, but the cot bed is a wonderful half-way house. The child feels secure, whilst learning how not to roll out!

Children do love to share, so, if you are planning more children, or have twins, installing bunks saves space. These are built solidly as a permanent fixture, with useful shelves for night-time reading. Alternatively, buy bunks that can be split and separated as your children grow out of the novelty. Bunks are not a good idea for children under four years old, so you could remove the ladder and use the top bunk for storage until your child is old enough.

When buying a full-sized bed, invest in or borrow some bed guards to help him not to fall out for the first few months, and think about the practicalities. Children love to bounce on beds, no matter how much you try to discourage it, so a divan might be a better buy than a bed with legs and castors. A good bed should last a child well into his teens.

Think too about storage space: a divan with drawers is very useful. If space for guests is short in the rest of the house, consider buying a bed which has another that slips underneath, especially useful when your chil-

dren have friends over for the night. A bed need not be a totally serious business. If your child would love to sleep in a train or a boat, try out your creative skills by shaping bed ends and wheels from MDF (medium-density fibre board) using a jigsaw, then paint on a design. Prime/undercoat the wood, cover it in a matt base coat, and draw out the design in pencil first, using the technique described on page 27.

As your child moves from cot to bed, starts to attend nursery, then school, the decor will change with him. You can phase out babyish pictures, move soft toys, and replace the oddments of baby-hood with pinboards, a clock as he learns to tell the time, pictures he has painted him-self, a piggy bank, all the accoutrements of growing up.

The baby changing area can become a desk or dressing table top. Frilly baskets and lacy pillows can be replaced with toy boxes and scatter cushions, covered in classic fabrics which will last through to the teenage years.

Right: **The cot has been removed, and this room has grown with the child. The shelves are used for toys rather than nappies, and there is room for toys and a small but sturdy child-sized desk and chair. The classic gingham fabric, which looked pretty when the room was a nursery, has stood up to the transition.**

Below: **This beautiful bed, though expensive, will serve a child for years. It begins life as a cot, graduates into a child's bed, and finally turns into a sofa for a teenager's room.**

The playroom/bedroom

If the room is going to serve for sleeping and playing, plan the space so that the sleeping area can remain free of clutter.

Allocate a wall for creativity, and perhaps cover it with a blackboard or cork tiles. Even if you decide to leave this wall plain, allow it to become a place for hanging or sticking pictures. If you encourage your child to use this area to show off his artistic skills, he is less likely to become creative on the other walls. It is also a good idea to include an easel on an area of floor which is washable.

There is a good argument at this time for buying a scaled-down table and chair, where the toddler can sit, with his feet touching the floor, to draw or scribble. Plastic ones will do fine. If you decide to buy a full-sized desk and chair that will serve in later years, make sure it is sturdy enough to allow a small child to climb on to it without fear of it tipping over. Bean bags are fun for children, who can lie in them for stories, or throw them at each other without causing too much damage!

Toys need to be easy to reach, and cupboard doors easy to open and close. Colourful plastic stacker boxes are very practical (mark each one with its contents, e.g., a simple train image for the train set, for the pre-reading child), as are wooden boxes which can be pulled around the room on castors.

Desirable toys placed high up on shelves are a recipe for disaster as a child will do almost anything to reach them.

The pre-school child enjoys bright, fun pictures and patterns around his room, which need not be expensive. Add colour with toys, cushions, pictures in bright frames or boxes painted with fun characters. Bed linen too can be fun, now he is old enough for a pillow and duvet. There are a great many designs on the market, or you could make sheets and duvet covers yourself, using cotton sheeting, which is available in a variety of patterns and colours from good fabric retailers. A child soon adds his own colour, in the shape of pictures from playgroup, masterpieces of Mummy or Daddy, and scribbles which don't look much, but which mean a great deal to him.

These colourful drawers are easy for little fingers to open, and deep enough to store plenty of toys.

A room will grow with your child so the fabric you choose should grow with him too.

The school-aged child

Once your child begins school, his or her needs change. There are still toys, but they become more sophisticated. Teddies are replaced by construction sets and train tracks; doll's houses are replaced by cassette players; scribbles give way to proper pictures. The sex of the child will be much more in evidence in the style of the room – up until this age, young children enjoy much the same sort of toys and games (except perhaps for dolls).

You need to provide more storage space as the number of accoutrements grows with your child. He needs a desk for homework, though, in the early days, you may prefer him to work near you. The desk need not be a ready-made one: two small matching chests of drawers with a table top laid on them will do just as well, or a small wooden or plastic table. Whatever you choose must be strong, and high enough for knees to get underneath. A comfortable chair is important, as is adequate lighting. Choose an anglepoise or desk lamp which throws a good amount of light.

The most important transition during these growing years is the discovery that your child has his own opinions about the space where he lives and sleeps. No longer will you have exclusive say about decoration, and, if you let your child be involved in decisions, you may be able to come to a compromise with which you are both happy.

School-aged children need a desk for homework, but it need not be a conventional one. Here, a plain table with useful drawers has been painted to match the bed linen and fabric. Make sure furniture is clean before painting, by rubbing it down with furniture cleaner and a rag. Prime/undercoat the wood, then paint it in an eggshell-finish non-toxic paint (in this case stripes), waiting until the previous colour has dried before starting on the next. Keep lines straight using masking tape. Cover the finished piece with two coats of acrylic non-yellowing varnish to protect it against knocks and scratches. Include pots for storing pens and rulers, and a good source of lighting such as an anglepoise lamp.

A bedroom needs to be a fun place to play or relax, and you will need to allow for your child's views about how it is decorated.

Children's rooms offer a wonderful opportunity for fun with furniture. Bedside tables, wastepaper baskets and cupboard fronts need not escape a paint brush and a bit of imagination. You could use stamps and stencils too (see page 58 for stencilling techniques). Take ideas for images from fabrics and pictures already in the room.

Storage

Obviously a growing child needs more space for clothes. A larger chest of drawers will do the job, but if you don't already have a wardrobe, it may be time to install one. You could split it so that half the wardrobe is taken with shelves, half with hanging space. As a small child's clothes won't hang to the floor, you could install two hanging rails, one under the other, to use the space most economically. The bottom of the hanging area is useful for boxes of toys. Young children love toys and games with small components (tiny construction sets, board games and jigsaws, dolls' clothes), so colourful boxes, with the contents marked, helps to encourage some sort of order.

The toy basket is still useful for soft toys and dolls. Some space could be given over to storage for dressing-up clothes, and an umbrella stand is ideal for tennis rackets or cricket bats.

As a child grows, he collects more books and needs space to store them. Intersperse them with ornaments, traditional wooden toys, or photographs for interest. A message board or cork board stores mementos neatly and safely, once a child is old enough to be trusted with drawing pins.

Right: **Where space is short for shelves, this fabric system threads onto a wardrobe pole and keeps clothes, toys or tapes close at hand and easy to reach.**
Below: **Though you can't expect it to be packed away neatly every evening, a canvas toy box like this one stores old toys and games tidily under a bed or at the bottom of a cupboard. Look for space opportunities under windows too. A window box would store old clothes, books and bedding, and, with a cushion on top, provides a seat or a place for displaying favourite soft toys.**

41

Sharing

Many children enjoy the company of a shared room, and space restrictions may mean you have no other choice. But once children begin to grow, they need privacy and an area to call their own. Try to arrange furniture so that desks and beds are not next to each other, and give each child his own bedside table, bookshelves, or part of a wardrobe. Consider partially splitting the room with a bookshelf, chair, curtain or sofa.

Lighting should be separate too, especially if children are of different ages, so that one can read while the other is asleep.

Toys

There are as many varieties of toys as there are children, and your child will have particular toys which have become very special. His interest will wax and wane too, so, just because he seems to lose interest in something he was mad about, or if he shows little interest in a birthday toy, do not despair. Simply put it away for a few weeks, and then introduce it again when he is looking for new stimulation.

There are certain toys, however, which have a universal appeal, and in which you might consider investing for your child's room. It is not always necessary to

buy a manufactured version, as copies of classic toys are often just as good and much cheaper.

Doll's house

These continue to charm children of all ages, and not just little girls. You can be as extravagant as you please, but many children are very happy playing with a house (or castle or fort) made from a sturdy cardboard box, which they have painted themselves. Large cardboard boxes which have contained household appliances such as refrigerators or chest freezers make marvellous play houses – ask for empty boxes at an electrical store.

Train set

Setting up a 'permanent' train track avoids having to put it away every night. Make a base from plywood or MDF (medium-density fibre board) and spray with non-toxic paint of the type recommended for use on children's furniture. When the base is dry, set up the track, then glue it in place piece by piece, using rubber-based glue sparingly (again of the type safe for children), so that it will withstand knocks, but can be dismantled eventually without damage to the track or base. Now build a 'scene' around the track, making a cardboard station from an old shoe box, adding farm animals, and trees cut from card and painted. Another idea is to paint cork floor tiles with a 'road network', or a farm with fields and ponds.

Kitchen or work bench

Role playing is fun, as well as educational, and several companies make workbenches, kitchens, hairdressers' shops in bright solid plastic. You could create your own kitchen or workbench from plywood or MDF. Make a table (jointed with screws) and a back piece for hanging toy utensils or tools from chunky plastic hooks. Paint or spray using paint approved for use on children's furniture. For a kitchen, paint four circles on the work surface for a hob, and make a hinged oven door, including a knob (see drawing).

NOTE: When making furniture for children, sand all edges until rounded and smooth.

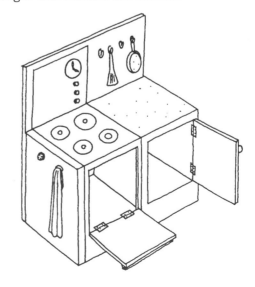

4 Rooms for teenagers

Many parents describe the teenage years as the most difficult. Your child has grown up, has a mind and a will of his own, yet he is still young enough to be living at home and in need of your guidance, however subtly given.

A teenager's room can be the most contentious battleground. He will see it as his space where he can be alone, take his friends, do what he likes. You will see it as a place which is still part of your home. Work together to create a room which takes into account both opinions, aiming for a compromise which leaves you happy with the room, and your teenager feeling that his or her opinions are being respected.

The teenager's point of view

Once a child becomes a teenager, his or her room takes on a whole new role. It is time to pack away the things of childhood. Teenagers have a right to some of the privileges adults enjoy, including a place of their own, decorated in a grown-up style.

The ideal room for teenagers is the bedroom-cum-study-cum-living room, where they can listen to their music and entertain their friends, without interference from parents. It may be time to move your child's room completely, perhaps by altering the layout of the house. Could you extend your home in

The teenager's ideal room will combine bedroom, study and a place to entertain friends.

some way? Is there space in the roof for a loft conversion to make another room? Could you move to a bigger house where your teenager can have more space?

Whether you decide on major changes, or to adapt the child's existing room, the choice of decoration may be a battleground. The fact that you have a taste for chintz does not mean this will be acceptable to your teenager. Compromising on style and taste is the order of the day.

By the teenage years, girls' and boys' ideas on decoration differ radically. This is the time to allow your child to express his masculinity or her femininity. Boys need space which is functional. The hi-fi or CD player is important, and he may need an area for construction hobbies. He may well want to hang scale models from the ceiling, or have a football table permanently erected.

Girls like a dressing table, small pots for storing the minutiae which fascinates this age group: hair ties, jewellery, make-up. Girls are often less keen to part with childhood toys, so the doll's house or soft toys may need a permanent home.

Your point of view

It is often helpful to agree boundaries of behaviour and to set a few ground rules. Agree that you will be content with changes in decoration, on condition that the room is kept relatively tidy and clean. You could set times when loud music is not permitted, when younger siblings are doing homework or going to bed, for example. Where safety is concerned, the rules must be strict.

• Candles and cigarettes are a large fire risk and should not be allowed in a bedroom where there are mattresses and cushions.

• Make sure you have provided enough electric sockets for the hi-fi, television, computer, and electronic musical instruments.

• If you are allowing a kettle in the room, make sure it is plugged in on a suitable surface, away from the edge of a table or sideboard, and away from fabrics and flammable items.

Furniture

When creating a lovely room for your teenager, select furniture which is sophisticated enough to reflect the adult he or she wants to be.

Bed

A childhood bedhead can be dispensed with, or replaced with an adult version. Cover the bed with a washable cover or quilt, and use scatter cushions to provide extra seating in the daytime. If your teenager has friends to stay overnight, buy an extra mattress to slide under the bed, or invest in a bed which has an integral weekend bed underneath. A futon might replace the bed completely, and if there is space, an armchair or small sofa will make a comfortable place for reading, as will big cushions or bean bags on the floor. A hammock suspended securely across the corner of the room adds a fun touch.

Flooring

This is a good time to lay a carpet if you have had vinyl or wooden flooring up to now. Teenagers can be trusted more than small children with carpeting (just!), and carpet makes the room cosier. Brightly coloured rugs will make a room feel more like a sitting-room.

Desk

Your teenager needs a desk big enough to spread out books and papers. It need not be a conventional office desk, as a good-sized table or wide shelf attached to the wall will do. On the other hand, it helps to encourage an organised approach (and creates the feeling that you are taking him or her seriously) if you provide enough shelves for books and files, space for the computer if there is one, pots for pens and rulers, and a small set of drawers for storing work. Office furniture and accessories, such as lever arch files (available in bright colours), boxes and filing systems, all help to create a grown-up look.

Lighting needs to be sufficient, with a good anglepoise lamp over the desk. Main lighting could be on a dimmer switch to make it softer. The chair used for homework must be the correct height for the desk, and comfortable.

Right: **Mirrors, especially full-length ones, are an essential part of growing up – teenagers are fascinated by their looks.**

Below: **The blue room looks fresh and easy to keep clean, an important consideration with teenagers. Boys and girls need lots of storage space, a desk, and a chair or comfortable bed to relax on.**

Above: **Teenagers want to express their personalities in their rooms. Girls often surround themselves with soft, feminine colours and fabrics, and need lots of storage space for favourite toys and the growing number of clothes.**

Left: **Boys like more functional space. Here a wide shelf desk provides space for homework and model building.**

Above: **When space is short, teenagers may have to share a room. These two single beds have been given a more sophisticated look by adding unusual detail around the four posters. The rest of the room is kept simple to prevent it looking cluttered. Where a room is very small, a place for doing homework may have to be found elsewhere in the house.**

Right: **Teenagers need a desk which provides enough space, even if it is unconventional. In a small room, a triangle of MDF (medium-density fibre board) fitted across a corner then painted is ideal. Matching shelves above provide space for books and files. (See Chapter 5 for how to make them.)**

A row of plain wooden pegs running the length of a wall is ideal for hanging a sports kit, or school bag.

Storage

Teenagers acquire more and more possessions. Clothes and shoes become a fascination, and wardrobe space needs to be adequate (not just for girls). Plenty of drawer space is needed for scarves, belts and underwear. Put hooks on the backs of doors for coats, and, for the sake of cleanliness, keep football boots and sports kit in a plastic storage box. Try to be ruthless about removing clothes once they are too small. Sell them or store them in clean bags or boxes in the roof, or at the bottom of a little-used cupboard.

When space is very short, it may help to raise the child's bed onto a platform, with drawer space beneath. Most children love the novelty of a platform bed.

Book shelves need to be copious. Accessories and ornaments will find a home here, as well as school books and novels, and any collections your child may have started. Your teenager may well play a musical instrument and need a safe place to store it. It is worth considering covering a whole wall in a modular shelving unit, where the shelf sizes can be adjusted, and the hi-fi can be stored at eye or waist level, with the wires tucked safely behind. CDs and tapes can be stored on shelves around the sound system itself. Leave a space beneath the shelves for a desk and chair, so that books can be reached easily when their owner is seated at the desk.

If your teenager has a television in his room, place it on a small chest of drawers in which tapes and videos can be stored, or invest in boxes made especially for that purpose.

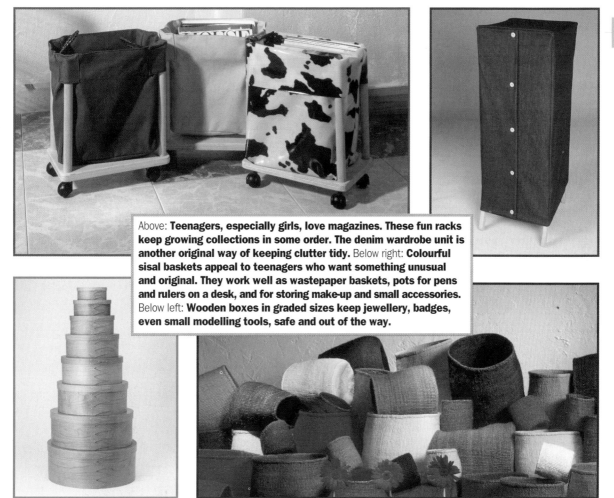

Above: **Teenagers, especially girls, love magazines. These fun racks keep growing collections in some order. The denim wardrobe unit is another original way of keeping clutter tidy.** Below right: **Colourful sisal baskets appeal to teenagers who want something unusual and original. They work well as wastepaper baskets, pots for pens and rulers on a desk, and for storing make-up and small accessories.** Below left: **Wooden boxes in graded sizes keep jewellery, badges, even small modelling tools, safe and out of the way.**

Details for a teenager's room

The classic fabric you chose for your small child may well have outgrown its usefulness, and your teenager will have his or her own opinions about decor.

Fashions change like the wind, so, for curtains or drapes, choose a cheap fabric which can be changed as your child changes his or her mind, or make a decision together on a more grown-up fabric, such as in this photo. Alternatively, hang neutral curtains and have more fun with wall colour, bed linen, valances and cushions. Teenagers enjoy dark colours on the walls (perhaps you should draw the line at black), but deep cerise pinks, ochres, greens and blues can be very effective, so long as there is enough light.

Unusual textures in fabrics and ornaments help to make the room more individual. A bed looks feminine and romantic with a muslin canopy suspended over it (see Chapter 5 for how to make one). Velvet or silk covered cushions look luxurious for relatively little money (they can be made from half a metre of fabric).

53

Glass beads and pebbles provide visual interest as does a shelf full of jewel-coloured bottles and pots.

Older teenagers, especially girls, adore the outrageous and even the kitsch, from bright paper lampshades to gold Cupids, candlesticks, beads and bangles. Plants, especially more exotic ones, add a sophisticated look to a teenager's room, and he or she might enjoy the responsibility of looking after them. Thankfully, such accessories are comparatively inexpensive and can make the difference between a boring bedroom and a room to impress friends!

The bright picture frames bought for the nursery are still useful. You may be able to simply change the images in them. Teenagers like to have photos around, and both sexes love posters. You will have to turn a blind eye to their choice of wall covering – this is where your taste is bound to be on a collision course with theirs – but persuading them to use Blu-Tack may protect the walls from the onslaught.

Brightly coloured walls, with contrasting cushions and bed linen, make a lively room which a teenager will enjoy.

Above: **Indian cotton throws and cushions are an inexpensive way to give a room an ethnic feel. Use baskets and large floor cushions to complete the look.**

Bottom left: **Contrast colours with inexpensive details like linen and paint**

Bottom right: **The valance on this bed is hung with an unusual button detail. The tabs are looped over the struts of the bed.**

5 Details for children's rooms

While the rest of your house can remain the same for years, a child's room changes as he grows. Take care that these changes are not too costly. The basics (the expensive part), such as flooring, paintwork and larger pieces of furniture, need never change. As the child develops, you can change the smaller details yourself, following these step-by-step guidelines.

Furniture

Shelves above a bed are ideal for children, especially if you want to encourage early wakers to play and read until the rest of the world surfaces. These shelves (**left**) have been fitted in an unusual way across a corner, but they are easy to make and install.

1. Cut a template out of cardboard, to the size and shape you want the shelves to be. Draw around your template on to MDF (medium-density fibre board, available at D.I.Y. stores in a variety of thicknesses).

2. Using a saw or jigsaw and the template, cut as many shelves as you need.

3. Sand the edges so they are rounded, and fix the shelves to the wall by screwing them onto small battens fixed to the wall with screws. Make sure the battens are thick enough to take the weight of the shelf. You can vary the space between each shelf, to fit what will be displayed on them.

4. Paint the shelves once they are in situ. Make sure the surface is clean and dust free. Prepare with primer/undercoat, and then use a top coat of emulsion or eggshell. You might want to add visual detail in a different colour on the edge of the shelves, once the top coat is dry. Fix with varnish if the shelves will be knocked frequently.

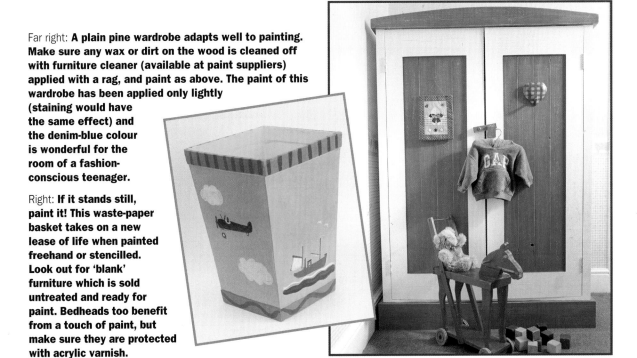

Far right: **A plain pine wardrobe adapts well to painting. Make sure any wax or dirt on the wood is cleaned off with furniture cleaner (available at paint suppliers) applied with a rag, and paint as above. The paint of this wardrobe has been applied only lightly (staining would have the same effect) and the denim-blue colour is wonderful for the room of a fashion-conscious teenager.**

Right: **If it stands still, paint it! This waste-paper basket takes on a new lease of life when painted freehand or stencilled. Look out for 'blank' furniture which is sold untreated and ready for paint. Bedheads too benefit from a touch of paint, but make sure they are protected with acrylic varnish.**

Stencilling is an easy and effective way to decorate a child's room. Infants love animals or soldiers marching around their rooms, teenagers enjoy geometric patterns, leaves or flowers. If you feel inspired, cut your own stencil from acetate or oiled stencil card, using a sharp scalpel, perhaps a pattern or image which already appears in the room. For the less confident, there are a huge number of stencils on the market, often in complete packs which include the correct brushes and paints.

Almost any surfaces can be stencilled, including walls, floors, fabric or furniture, so long as they are not glossy or shiny.

Whether you are stencilling a wall frieze, or a simple pattern like the one on these drawers, you need to measure out the pattern so that the spacing is regular. Using a stencil cut from acetate is probably the easiest option because it allows you to see through the stencil to where the pattern will appear. It can be wiped clean too. Use oil- or water-based paint, even emulsion will do. Use fast drying fabric paint when stencilling fabric, and coloured wood stain or gloss for floors and furniture (sealing it with acrylic varnish).

1. If you are cutting your own stencil, cut the larger shapes first, securing the acetate with tape. When cutting shapes, turn the stencil, not the knife. Cut a separate stencil if you are planning to use more than one colour, and mark each piece of film with a registration mark at the top, or at each corner.

2. If you are stencilling a border, use a spirit level to ensure lines are straight. Even more random designs will need planning and measuring out to keep them regular.

3. Tape the stencil to the surface with masking tape each time you use it to avoid slippage, and use the paint sparingly, whether you are using traditional blunt stencilling brushes, or a small sponge (easier on larger surfaces like walls and floors). It helps to dab most of the paint off onto scrap paper before applying the brush/sponge to the stencil.

4. Leave the stencil on for a short time before lifting it and moving on, and make sure one colour is completely dry before starting the next.

NOTE: Keep a tissue moistened with solvent close by to wipe off mistakes, and clean your stencil regularly to avoid smudging.

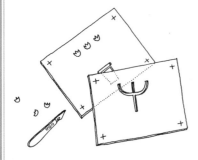

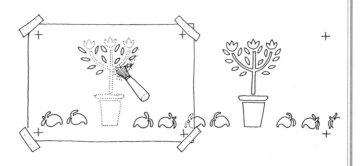

Fabrics

A pretty frill for the top of a table or chest looks attractive, and helps to protect the furniture from marks and splashes.

1. Measure the top of the table or chest, and cut a piece of fabric to that size, adding 1cm all round for the seam. For the corners, place a saucer at the corner of the fabric and cut around it to get a rounded shape.

2. For the frill, measure the distance around the four edges of the table or chest top. Cut a length of fabric twice this measurement (probably several pieces joined together) and 10cm wide (or the depth of frill required plus 2cm).

3. Turn and stitch a 1cm hem along one long edge of frill.

4. Stitch a gathering stitch 1cm in along the other long edge of the frill and gently gather the frill until it fits around the table or chest top, allowing 1cm at each end of the frill to join the two ends together.

5. Stitch enough binding cord into a casing of contrasting fabric, place the frill and top piece right sides together, with the binding cord sandwiched between, and stitch through all four layers, finishing off by tucking in the binding cord neatly.

NOTE: Make sure the fabric you choose is washable, and wash it before sewing, to avoid shrinkage afterwards. You may want to starch the fabric for a crisper edge.

Left: **These ends for a curtain pole would delight any car-crazy little boy. Once the novelty wears off they can be removed to leave a simple pole.**

Below: **A plain box pelmet or bedhead can be livened up with simple stuffed shapes, such as stars, moons, and suns, in contrasting fabric. (See page 26 'Making a Mobile', for details on how to make these soft shapes.) Attach them by sticking or sewing Velcro to the pelmet (sticking is less permanent) and the shape itself.**

Even very young girls love the romance of a muslin canopy over their bed. Use undyed muslin (you may need three widths for a single bed) long enough to fall to the floor and to fit round the bed generously, leaving a gap of 10cm between the bed and the canopy. Stitch the muslin panels using flat seams, leaving most of one side open and hemmed. Canopies are most effective when gathered and suspended from a ceiling hook, and over a hoop hanging from the same hook (use strong nylon thread).

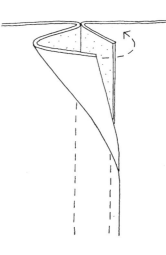

You will need:
• rectangle of fabric twice the length of the bag you want to make. Allow 1.5cm seam allowance down each side, and 4cm at each end for a small bag, 6cm for a larger one
• thick cord (in proportion to the size of the bag) measuring twice the width of the bag, plus about 30cm

1. Cut a rectangle of fabric the width of the bag required, and twice the length (plus seam allowance).
2. Fold the fabric right sides together and press. Then mark a point 4 or 6cm down from the top (depending on the heading allowance) on both sides and make a horizontal cut 1.5cm into the fabric at these points.
3. Turn in 1cm of the top and side edges above the cuts and hem.
4. Turn down the top edge of the heading, until just beyond the cuts. Stitch from cut to cut across the bag close to the edge and then again 2 or 3cm up from this line to form a casing for the cord. (The size of the casing will depend on the thickness of the cord.)
5. Stitch the side edges of the bag up to the cuts, turning the seam in 0.5cm then again 1cm. Turn the bag right sides out.
6. Thread the cord through the casing, both sides of the bag, and tie a knot where the two ends meet.
NOTE: For added detail, sew tassels at the bottom corners, stitch the child's name or a fabric motif to the front of the bag, or put interesting toggles at the end of the cord.

Drawstring bags in a variety of sizes are useful to a child of any age, for storing sports kit, toys, hair ties and hair bands, diaries and books, even laundry. They are easy to make and look wonderful in bright fabrics, checks, stripes, and zigzags. Any fabric will do, but for laundry or sports bags use a strong washable cotton.

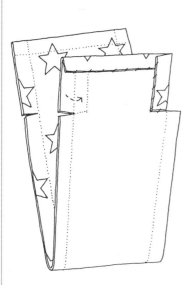
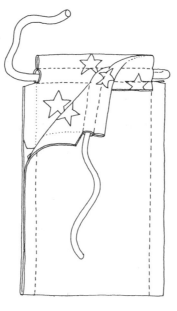

Collections

Children love to make collections, which can be added to as a result of school trips, holidays or presents from family and friends. Building a collection need not be an expensive business – boxes, wooden or china pigs, old toy cars, plastic soldiers are easy to come by for little money.

These wooden fish are relatively inexpensive, and come in bright fun colours. Soft toys come in a variety of sizes and prices. The collection can grow in value and sophistication as the child grows up. Old-fashioned dressing-table bottles are harder to find

but look pretty in a child's room, as do rarer tin soldiers or china dolls. A collection begun in childhood can continue to be enjoyed right into adulthood.

Display collections at their best by allocating shelf space or a table top (making sure you've allowed for the collection to grow). These soft toys look effective (and stay tidy) displayed in an old doll's pram.

Special touches for children's rooms

• Book-ends come in all sorts of weird and wonderful designs, from sleeping frogs to flying cows, and are a lovely way to keep children's books tidy.

• Clocks and calendars are useful for children learning to tell the time and date, and imperative for tardy teenagers. The styles and designs are endless.

• Height charts made from paper or wood are fun in small children's rooms and enable you to mark milestones in growth from the moment your child can stand.

• Wipe-clean colouring posters are available from toy shops, with special felt-tip pens. Keep a poster pinned to a washable area of wall, and the child can colour and clean off mistakes at will.

• A basketball hoop or dart board provides hours of entertainment on wet days. Hang it from the side of a wardrobe, or on an area of wall where there is plenty of space, away from breakable objects.

• A globe or abacus is not expensive and can provide amusement for even very young children.

Acknowledgements

There are a large number of childcare companies who supply furniture, bedding and accessories for children's bedrooms, and it is worth looking beyond these specialists for unusual ideas. The following companies have been kind enough to supply pictures of their products for this book.

Cosatto: cot and cot bed, pages 19, 30–31. Tel: 01268 727070 for nearest stockist.

Early Learning Centre: cot and furniture, pages 10, 14–15, 22–23, 29. Tel: 0990 352352.

Habitat: furniture, pages 45, 47. Tel: 0171 255 2545 for nearest store.

The Hill Toy Company: doll's house and train set, pages 42, 43. Tel: 01765 689955 for mail-order catalogue.

The Holding Company: caterpillar cot bumper, magazine racks and sisal baskets, pages 24, 51. Tel: 0171 610 9160 for mail-order catalogue.

Lido Mail Order: toy box and denim wardrobe, pages 41, 51. Tel: 01702 77928 for mail-order catalogue.

Mothercare: safety products, page 9, 10. Tel: 01923 210210 for your nearest store.

The Pier: fabric shelving system, mirrors, throws, and fish, pages 41, 47, 55, 63. Tel: 0171 351 7100 for nearest stockist.

Shaker Mail Order: wooden boxes, page 51. Tel: 0171 724 7672 for catalogue.

Simon Horn Furniture: cot bed, page 33. Tel: 0171 731 1279.

First published in 1997 by Boxtree
an imprint of Macmillan Publishers Ltd
25 Eccleston Place, London SW1W 9NF
and Basingstoke
Associated companies throughout the world

ISBN 0 7522 1105 6

Text © Boxtree, an imprint of Macmillan Publishers Ltd 1997
Photographs © IPC Magazines Ltd

The right of Annie Ashworth to be identified as Author of this Work has been asserted by her in accordance with the Copyright, Designs and Patents Act 1988.

1 3 5 7 9 8 6 4 2

A CIP catalogue entry for this book is available from the British Library.

Front cover photographs by: main picture, Lewis Tikly; insets, Bill Reavell, reproduced courtesy of *Homes & Ideas* magazine and Robert Harding Syndication

Designed by Robert Updegraff
Illustrations by Julia Glynn-Smith
Printed and bound in Italy by Manfrini

Children's Rooms is one of a series of books published in association with *Homes & Ideas* magazine. Also available are: *Shelving and Storage*, *Window Dressing* and *Floors and Flooring*. All the books in the series are available from bookshops, recommended retail price £4.99, or you can order direct from the publisher: Boxtree, an imprint of Macmillan General Books C. S., Book Service by Post, PO Box 29, Douglas I-O-M, IM99 1BQ; tel: 01624 675137; fax: 01624 670923; Internet: http://www.bookpost.co.uk. There is a charge of 75 pence per book for postage and packing. Overseas customers please allow £1.00 per copy for post and packing.

Homes & Ideas is published monthly by Southbank Publishing Group, IPC Magazines Ltd, King's Reach Tower, Stamford Street, London SE1 9LS. For subscription enquiries and overseas orders call 01444–445555 (fax no: 01444–445599). Please send orders, address changes and all correspondence to: IPC Magazines Ltd, Oakfield House, 35 Perrymount Road, Haywards Heath, West Sussex RH16 3DH. All cheques should be made payable to IPC Magazines Ltd. Alternatively, you can call the subscription credit card hotline (UK orders only) on 01622–778778.